SPECTRUM®
READERS

D1551097

3

DISCOVER!
Washington, D.C.

By Teresa Domnauer

Carson-Dellosa
Publishing

An imprint of Carson-Dellosa Publishing, LLC
P.O. Box 35665
Greensboro, NC 27425-5665

carsondellosa.com

Printed in the USA. All rights reserved.
ISBN 978-1-4838-0129-2

01-002141120

Washington, D.C., is the capital of the United States of America.

The District of Columbia (D.C.) is a territory, not a state.

Washington, D.C., is home to the federal, or national, government.

Millions of visitors come here to see monuments and museums.

Millions more live, work, and play here.

Washington, D.C., is a fascinating city to discover!

A Busy City

Washington, D.C., is found on the east coast of the United States.

The Potomac (puh TOE mick) River separates it from the state of Virginia. Each day, over one million people go to work here in offices, government buildings, and foreign embassies.

Many travel through Union Station by train and ride the underground Metro. When they are not working, people gather in the city for celebrations and festivals.

Fascinating Facts

- Streets in Washington, D.C., are named by letters and numbers arranged in a grid.
- About half the land in Washington, D.C., is owned by the U.S. government.

National Mall

A long, wide green space runs through Washington, D.C.

This is the National Mall.

It has been called *America's front lawn*.

Museums, historical monuments, parks, and memorials line the Mall.

At different times, Americans come here to picnic, watch fireworks, listen to speakers and concerts, and witness presidential inaugurations.

Fascinating Facts

- Over 20,000 trees grow along the Mall and in the Memorial Parks.
- Each spring, colorful kites fly over the Mall during the Blossom Kite Festival.

White House

The White House is the office and home of the president of the United States. Its address is 1600 Pennsylvania Avenue, Washington, D.C. The grand house has 132 rooms, with 35 bathrooms and 28 fireplaces on six floors. The president's famous Oval Office is found in the West Wing. The president's family lives in a private part of the building.

Fascinating Facts

- The first president to live in the White House was President John Adams in 1800.
- The White House has its own tennis court, swimming pool, and bowling lane.

U.S. Capitol Building

The Rotunda, a round room with a magnificent decorated ceiling, lies under the famous dome of the U.S. Capitol. British troops set fire to the building during the War of 1812, but rain saved it. During the Civil War, soldiers slept inside. The U.S. congress has worked here for over 200 years to make laws for the nation.

Fascinating Facts

- The Rotunda is 180 feet tall!
- The U.S. Capitol has its own private subway.

Supreme Court Building

The massive marble Supreme Court Building was built in 1935.

Nine Supreme Court justices work here to decide the most important legal cases in the nation.

The building contains a main courtroom, offices, a library, and private rooms for the justices called *chambers*.

Fascinating Facts

- The Supreme Court library contains 500,000 books.

- Bronze doors on the building weigh six and one-half tons each. That's more than four cars!

13

National Museum of Natural History

A giant stuffed elephant greets visitors to the National Museum of Natural History. Exhibits here show insects, dinosaurs, mammals, gems, and other objects from the natural world.

The museum is part of the Smithsonian Institution, a group of famous museums that has been called *America's attic*. Admission to the museums is free.

Fascinating Facts

- The Hope Diamond, one of the largest blue diamonds in the world, can be found here.
- The museum's collection includes over seven million kinds of fish!

Washington Monument

The Washington Monument was built to honor President George Washington. At 555 feet, it is taller than the Statue of Liberty!

Its famous shape, called an *obelisk*, is built of granite and marble.

The monument has 897 steps, but an elevator can take visitors to the top in just a little over a minute.

Fascinating Facts

- It took 36 years to complete the Washington Monument.
- The monument suffered damage from an earthquake in August 2011.

Cherry Blossom Festival

In 1912, Japan gave over 3,000 cherry trees to the city as a gift of friendship. The trees were planted throughout the National Mall and the Memorial Parks. Each spring, the trees bloom with thousands of pink flowers.
Starting in 1934, the arrival of the blossoms has been celebrated at the Cherry Blossom Festival.

Fascinating Facts

- The Japanese word for flowering cherry tree is *Sakura*.

- The Japanese government gave the United States another 3,800 cherry trees in 1965.

19

Jefferson Memorial

This monument honors Thomas Jefferson, the third president of the United States and author of the Declaration of Independence.

It was dedicated on April 13, 1943.

A statue of Jefferson stands inside.

Water in the Tidal Basin flows outside.

Fascinating Facts

- Thomas Jefferson would have turned 200 years old on the day the Jefferson Memorial was dedicated.

- The round monument with columns is modeled after the Pantheon, an ancient building in Rome.

Vietnam Veterans Memorial

The Vietnam Veterans War Memorial is also simply called *the wall*.
Designed by Maya Lin, this quiet place honors U.S. soldiers who died while fighting in the Vietnam War.
Their names are carved into 70 panels made of shiny, black granite.
People come to find the names of friends and family members who died.

Fascinating Facts

- There are over 58,000 names carved into the wall.
- The Vietnam War was fought from 1955 to 1975.

Lincoln Memorial

The Lincoln Memorial honors Abraham Lincoln, the 16th president.

Thirty-six marble columns surround an enormous statue of Lincoln.

A thoughtful, seated Lincoln looks out over the Reflecting Pool.

Two of Lincoln's famous speeches, including "The Gettysburg Address," are carved into the walls of the monument.

Fascinating Facts

- Martin Luther King, Jr. gave his famous "I Have a Dream" speech at the Lincoln Memorial in 1963.

- Lincoln's son Robert Todd Lincoln attended the dedication ceremony in 1922.

Arlington National Cemetery

Arlington, Virginia, lies across the Potomac River from Washington, D.C. Arlington National Cemetery is here. This is the resting place for more than 400,000 members of the U.S. military and their families.

Special remembrance services are held here on Memorial Day and Veterans Day. The vast cemetery covers over 600 acres.

Fascinating Facts

- The first military burial at Arlington took place on May 13, 1864 during the Civil War.
- Each year, three million people visit Arlington National Cemetery.

UNCOMMON
VALOR
WAS A COMMON
VIRTUE

Marine Corps War Memorial

The U.S. Marine Corps War Memorial is also located in Arlington, Virginia. It honors U.S. Marines who fought and died in a fierce battle on the tiny island of Iwo Jima, Japan, during World War II. The bronze statue shows six U.S. Marines raising the flag atop a mountain when the battle at Iwo Jima ended.

Fascinating Facts

- A famous photograph taken in 1945 inspired the memorial.
- Three soldiers from the photograph survived the war and served as models for the statue.

The Pentagon

The headquarters of the U.S. Department of Defense is also in Arlington, Virginia. The building is called the *Pentagon* because it has five wings, or sides. It is one of the largest office buildings in the world, with 23,000 workers! The Pentagon is like a small city—it has 16 parking lots, 131 stairways, 19 escalators, and over 17 miles of corridors.

Fascinating Facts

- The Army Corps of Engineers completed the Pentagon in 1943.

- There are over 16,000 light fixtures in the Pentagon, requiring 250 bulbs to be changed each day!

DISCOVER! Washington, D.C. Comprehension Questions

1. What street is the White House found on?

2. From what country did Washington, D.C., receive thousands of cherry trees?

3. What is the Vietnam Veterans War Memorial made from?

4. What branch of the U.S. government occupies the U.S. Capitol Building?

5. Which monuments honor former presidents of the U.S.?

6. What river is found between Washington, D.C., and Virginia?

7. How many justices work at the Supreme Court Building?

8. Which building is the headquarters of the Department of Defense?

9. What might you see along the National Mall?